BIGFOOT
AND OTHER MYSTERIES

John Townsend

CLASH

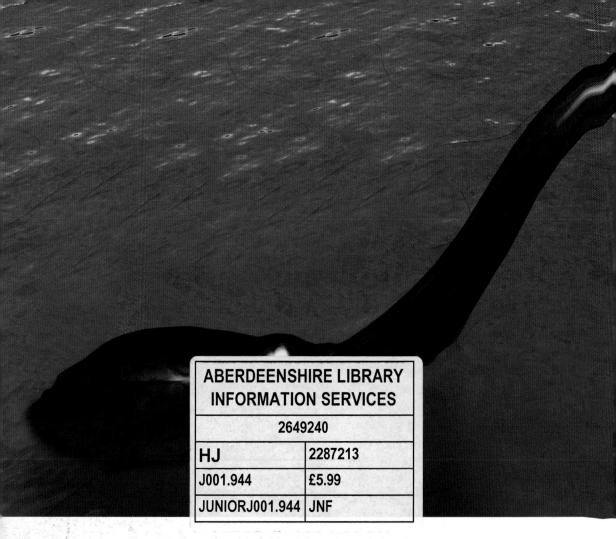

Copyright © ticktock Entertainment Ltd 2008

First published in Great Britain in 2008 by ticktock Media Ltd,
2 Orchard Business Centre, North Farm Road, Tunbridge Wells, Kent, TN2 3XF

project editor: Ruth Owen
ticktock project designer: Sara Greasley
ticktock picture researcher: Lizzie Knowles

With thanks to series editors Honor Head and Jean Coppendale.

Thank you to Lorraine Petersen and the members of nasen

ISBN 978 1 84696 747 4 pbk

Printed in China

Picture credits (t=top; b=bottom; c=centre; l=left; r=right):
AFP/Getty Images: 19t. Bryan & Cherry Alexander Photography/ Alamy: 17. Bettmann/CORBIS: 20, 21. Keystone/ Getty:
7t. Conrad Maufe/ naturepl.com: 10. Simon Mendez: 22-23. The Natural History Museum, London: 23c. Dale O'Dell /
Alamy: 1. Popperfoto/Getty Images: 19b. James Powell: OFC, 28t. Rex Features: 26-27. Seo75/ Wikimedia Commons:
31. Shutterstock: 2, 4, 5 both, 6-7, 8-9, 11t, 12-13, 14-15, 16, 28c, 29tl, 29br. John Sibbick/Fortean Picture Library: 24,
28b. Alistair Siddons / Alamy: 25. Wm. Leo Smith (1996): 11b. Topical Press Agency/ Getty Images : 18, 29tr.

Every effort has been made to trace copyright holders, and we apologise in advance for any omissions. We would be
pleased to insert the appropriate acknowledgments in any subsequent edition of this publication.

CONTENTS

SECRET BEASTS

Many places on Earth are wilderness.

Over half of the Earth is under deep water.

Do these secret places hide secret beasts?

You never know what may be
hiding nearby...watching.

It's time to take a closer look...

LOCH NESS MONSTER

For nearly 1,500 years, people have told stories of a secret beast in Scotland. They say it lives in a deep lake called Loch Ness.

In 1930, three young men were fishing on Loch Ness. Suddenly, a large creature swam towards their boat under the water.

The creature turned away about 300 metres from the boat. The fishermen were sure it was the Loch Ness Monster.

This famous photo of the monster was taken in 1934. However, it turned out to be a hoax. The monster was just a model!

In 1960, eyewitness Torquil MacLeod says he saw the Loch Ness Monster rise up out of the water.

He says the monster was 15 to 20 metres long. It had a neck like an elephant's trunk.

Does Loch Ness hide a secret beast?

KILLER KRAKEN

For hundreds of years, sailors told stories of a giant sea monster. It was called the Kraken.

The Kraken was believed to reach up from the deep ocean and attack ships.

SEA MONSTERS?

Could there be giant, monster-like creatures living in the ocean?

Perhaps the Kraken was actually a giant squid. These animals live deep under the sea.

Giant squid

Tentacles

This giant squid was washed up on a beach. They can grow much bigger than this, though!

A giant squid could cling to a boat with the suckers on its tentacles.

Suckers

Sailors say they have seen huge giant squid. They could not measure them, but they estimated their length was 18 to 20 metres. The squids' tentacles could be 5.5 metres long.

Perhaps some sea monsters were actually oarfish. This oarfish was washed up in California in 1996. It was 7.3 metres long.

TERROR BIRDS

Six million years ago, giant birds called teratorns flew over America. Teratorns had a wingspan like a small plane!

Some people say they have seen teratorns in modern times.

In July 1977, people say they saw two giant birds in the sky above Lawndale, Illinois, USA. The birds had wingspans of 8 metres.

Suddenly, one of the birds swooped down. It lifted ten-year-old Marlon Lowe off the ground. Marlon's mother ran to help. She screamed and the bird dropped the boy.

Some people think Marlon was attacked by a teratorn.

Others say it was a big, modern-day bird. But no modern-day bird has such a large wingspan.

Could teratorns still exist today?

PREHISTORIC BEASTS

In prehistoric times, flying reptiles called pterosaurs ruled the skies.

For many years, people in Texas, USA, have reported seeing these same beasts.

In 1982, James Thompson was driving in Texas. Suddenly, something huge swooped down low over the road.

The creature had a wingspan of at least 2 metres. There were no feathers on its wings – just skin.

When Thompson got home, he checked in a book. The book showed the beast was a pterosaur!

Could prehistoric pterosaurs still exist today?

MOUNTAIN BEAST

For years, the people who live in the mountains of Tibet and Nepal have talked of the Yeti.

The Yeti has long, dark hair.

It is 2 metres tall.

It walks like a human.

It also smells very bad!

In 2003, a girl in Nepal said she saw the Yeti.

The girl was looking after her yaks. She says the animals were attacked by the Yeti.

Yak

The Yeti was so strong it was able to rip the skin off the yaks. It even tore the legs off one yak.

The girl thought she was next. However, the beast disappeared back into the forest.

**Some people have seen Yeti footprints.
Others have tried to find the Yeti.**

In the 1930s, a team of men set off to climb Mount Everest in Nepal.

They saw huge footprints in the snow. Were they made by the Yeti?

The footprints were 33 centimetres long.

In 1971, an expedition set off to try to find the Yeti. The expedition was led by a Japanese Yeti hunter called Takahashi.

Takahashi says one of his men saw the Yeti.

" It looked like a gorilla. It stood on its back legs, like a man. Its head was covered with long, thick hair. It was not a bear or a monkey. "

Takahashi

At a monastery in Nepal, the monks have a huge scalp. They say it is the scalp of a Yeti.

Scalp

19

BIGFOOT

In the wild places of North America, there are stories of a beast called Bigfoot.

A scientist holds up casts of Bigfoot prints.

In 1967, a man named Roger Patterson filmed a Bigfoot in the north west of America.

The Bigfoot was over 2 metres tall.

It walked off towards some woods. Then it turned and looked towards Patterson.

This is a photo from Patterson's film. Some scientists say the film shows an unknown animal. Others say it is a man in an ape suit!

GIANT APES

Adult man

Gigantopithecus

Giant apes once lived on Earth.

The giant ape Gigantopithecus was
3 metres tall.

It lived until half a million years ago.

Scientists know about this giant ape
because they have found fossil teeth.

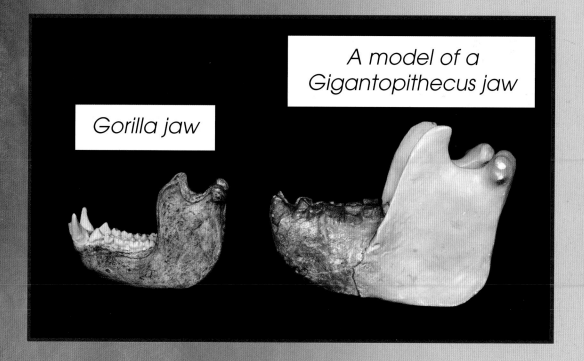

*A model of a
Gigantopithecus jaw*

Gorilla jaw

**Could the creatures known as Bigfoot
and the Yeti be Gigantopithecus?**

Could these giant apes
still be alive?

Spines

Chupacabra

Fangs

Leathery skin

24

NIGHT KILLER

In parts of North and South America, people say chupacabra attack goats, sheep and chickens at night.

People say chupacabras suck the animals' blood, and then leave them for dead.

What are chupacabras?

Some people say they were made in a science experiment. Then the killer beasts escaped from the science lab!

In 2006, Michelle O'Donnell of Maine, USA, found an animal hit by a car.

It was evil-looking with fangs. It looked like a dog. But not like any dog or wolf in the area!

GIANT SNAKES

Man's body

This giant anaconda was caught in 1990. It was **10 metres** long.

The snake had eaten a man!

Explorers in South American jungles say they have seen anacondas that are **30 metres** long.

None that big have been caught – yet!

A WORLD OF MYSTERY

Stories of strange beasts have been told around the world for hundreds of years. Could some of these beasts still be out there?

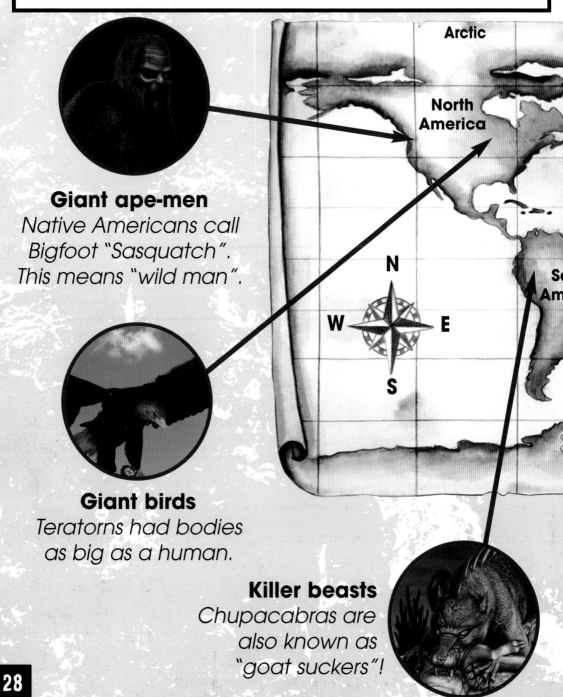

Giant ape-men
Native Americans call Bigfoot "Sasquatch". This means "wild man".

Giant birds
Teratorns had bodies as big as a human.

Killer beasts
Chupacabras are also known as "goat suckers"!

Arctic

North America

N

W · E

S

So
Am

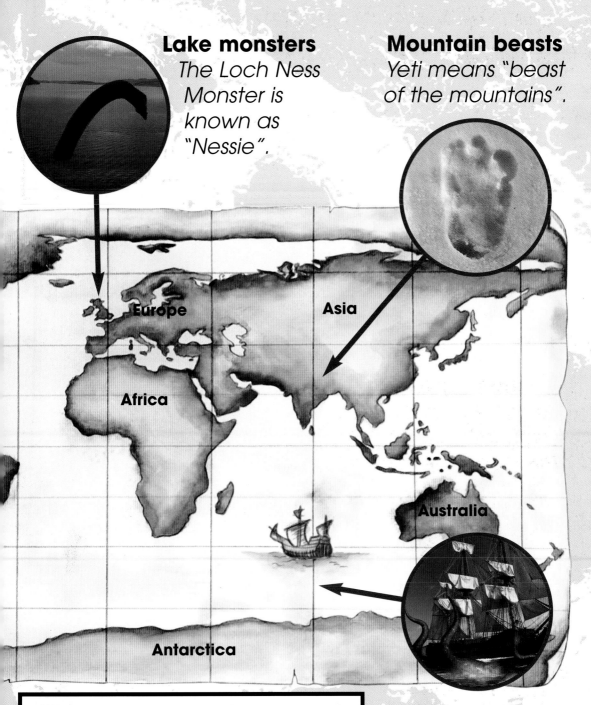

Lake monsters
The Loch Ness Monster is known as "Nessie".

Mountain beasts
Yeti means "beast of the mountains".

Europe

Asia

Africa

Australia

Antarctica

Perhaps there are even some beasts we don't know of yet. Keep watching.

They may be closer than you think...

Sea monsters
Giant squid can have eyes as big as dinner plates.

aboriginal The native people of Australia.

estimate To make a good guess using facts and eyewitness reports.

expedition A long journey that a person takes to find out information.

eyewitness A person who sees something happen.

fang A long, sharp tooth.

fossil A tooth or piece of bone that has turned into stone over millions of years.

hoax A practical joke.

monastery A place where monks and priests live and follow a religion.

Mount Everest The highest mountain in the world. It is 8,850 metres tall. Everest is on the border of China and Nepal.

oarfish A long fish with a thin, flat, ribbon-like body. People have reported seeing oarfish that were 17 metres long!

reptile A cold-blooded animal with a backbone. Snakes, lizards, turtles and crocodiles are all reptiles.

scalp The skin that covers the top of the head, with the hair attached.

tentacle A long body part that is used for touching and holding things.

wilderness An area in which few people live that is still in its natural state.

wingspan The measurement of a bird or plane's wings from wing tip to wing tip.

yak A hairy, plant-eating, mountain animal. People in Nepal and Tibet keep yaks for their milk, meat and skins.

MORE SECRET BEASTS

- For over 200 years, people have talked of "Chessie". They say this huge sea serpent lives around Chesapeake Bay on the east coast of the USA.

- In Australia, Aboriginal people talk of "Youree". It means "hairy man monster". The ape-man is also called Yowie. Not many people have seen Yowie. People say it is very shy. They also say that Yowie stinks!

A statue of Yowie

SECRET BEASTS ONLINE

Websites

http://www.unmuseum.org/lostw.htm

http://www.nessie.co.uk/

http://www.bfro.net/

INDEX